MASTER THE
BOW DRILL

An ancient tool by which a drill (also called a spindle) is turned using a string and bow to create enough friction to start a fire.

DROPSToNE PRESS
Pocket Field Guide: Master The Bow Drill
Creek Stewart

Copyright © 2016 by Creek Stewart
All Rights Reserved

Copyeditor: Jacob Perry

If you would like to do any of the above, please seek permission first by contacting us at http://www.dropstonepress.com

Wholesale inquiries please visit http://www.dropstonepress.com
Purchase this Pocket Field Guide and others in this series at
http://www.creekstewart.com

Published by DROPSToNE PRESS
ISBN 978-0-692-71955-8

dropstonepress.com

INTRODUCTION

There are few events in my life that I will never forget. Spinning out my first glowing, red-hot bow drill ember is one of them. There is something truly magical about the experience of rubbing two sticks together and creating fire. Without getting too philosophical, carving and using a bow drill kit takes us back in time.

It connects us to our distant ancestors who walked the earth thousands of years ago. When we make fire from the most basic of natural tools, we can't help but wonder what it must have been like to depend on such primitive technology for warmth, cooking, protection and our very survival.

The bow drill is without question the most famous of all survival friction fire-starting methods. Having taught this skill to thousands of students for more than two decades, I have concluded that mastering the bow drill teaches us much more than how to start a fire. Below is what you will learn from reading this pocket field guide and mastering the bow drill for yourself:

FIRST, carving a bow drill kit teaches knife proficiency. From notches and divots to batoning and sharpening, the finished bow drill kit requires you to learn many different carving techniques. I will describe all of these in detail. Expect to learn as much about your knife as you will about fire-making.

SECOND, sourcing bow drill components requires you to understand the properties of many different types of trees, shrubs and wild plants. To make a successful bow drill kit, you must first learn to identify the tree and plant resources in your surrounding environment.

THIRD, you will gain an intimate knowledge of fire, which modern fire-starting methods do not offer. If fire-starting were a 0-to-10 step process—0 being nothing and 10 being an open flame—most modern fire-starting tools would bump you to at least step 7.

Over the course of multiple steps, making fire with a bow drill will require you to create and coax a flame from a small, fragile, glowing-hot ember. More is learned about fire in this process than with any other fire-starting technique.

FINALLY, you will learn much about yourself, both physically and mentally. You'll be required to crouch on your knees and position your legs in specific ways while steadily pushing and pulling with your dominant arm for several minutes, which may prove uncomfortable and taxing. Mentally, your patience, perseverance and attention to detail will all be tested simultaneously. Regardless of these difficulties, the bow drill has the unique reputation for bringing about personal change and new perspectives. Hopefully, you too will add your first bow-drill ember to the short list of events never to be forgotten.

THE
BOW DRILL KIT

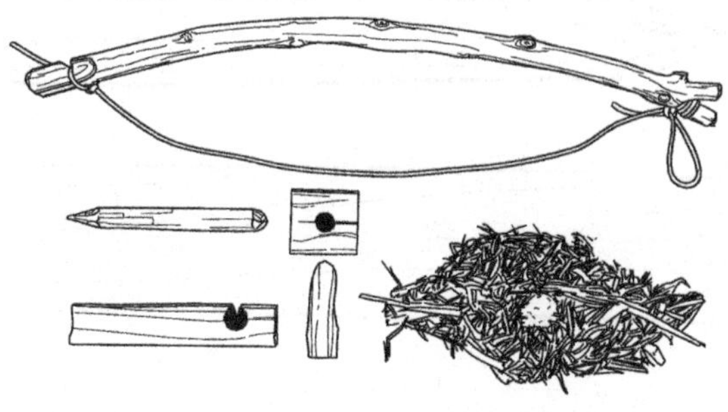

Throughout this guide I will be referencing the different components of a bow drill kit. The diagram above illustrates these components for your reference. This is what your finished kit will ultimately look like. Section titles correspond to the specific bow drill component names. The different components of a bow drill kit must be sourced from different types of woods according to the desired function. In each section I will detail the following:

- Component Description & Function
- Wood Properties & Selection
- Carving Instructions and Details

We'll start with the two most important components of any bow drill kit: *the spindle and hearth board.*

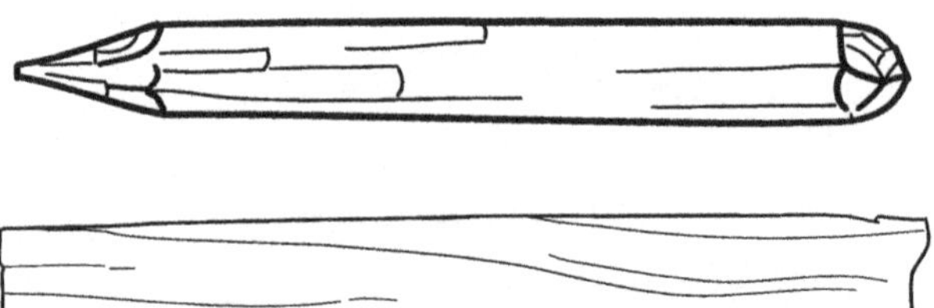

SPINDLE & HEARTH BOARD

> DESCRIPTION & FUNCTION

A string and bow are used to rotate the spindle into the hearth board. The fast-rotating spindle generates a fine dust at the point of contact with the hearth board. As this dust collects (and friction heat builds) it will develop into a smoldering ember.

If the wood you choose is not bone dry then you will not succeed in making fire with your bow drill kit. An ember can only be born in the near absence of moisture. For this reason, live green wood should never be used for the spindle or the hearth board. (*Live green wood is actually preferred for the bearing block, which we will discuss later.*)

If at all possible, wood for the spindle should not be gathered from the ground. With few environmental exceptions (such as extremely arid locales) wood found on the ground will be less desirable because it will have absorbed moisture. Dead standing wood and low-hanging branches are almost always drier because they are exposed to sun and wind.

EXPERT FIELD TIP

It can sometimes be difficult to determine by touch if a piece of wood is dry. I've found that the lips, cheeks and chin are more reliable than my fingertips in determining if a piece of wood contains moisture.

>> **WOOD TYPES**

Although I have successfully used many different types of wood for spindles, certain varieties work best. While I want you to be familiar with specific trees and plants that make excellent spindles, it's important that you first understand their key properties.

Soft and lightweight woods are preferred over hard and dense varieties. A popular rule of thumb is that you should be able to use your fingernail to make an indentation in the wood with little effort. While soft is preferred, the wood should not be "punky" or rotted. It should be firm.

I prefer to use the same exact type of wood for both the spindle and the hearth board. I've had the most success with this arrangement. Exceptions can be made, of course, but I prefer to cut both components from not only the same type of wood but the same piece of wood as well.

I also like to use tree branches and suckers (these are saplings growing from the base of larger trees) as op-posed to the main trunks. This faster-growth wood has a more porous texture than the dense, main trunk and creates a faster ember with less effort. Along that same line, I've found that the faster the tree grows, the better it is for bow drill spindles. Single-season growth is always an excellent choice. It just so happens that the tree varieties that work best for bow drills also grow extremely fast.

Finally, any wood you choose should be as straight as possible and free of knots or cracks.

>> Drying a Green Kit

You may not find dead, standing wood of the variety
you need, but you can cut live green wood and let it
dry. For one kit, I typically cut a branch or sucker
(preferred) about the diameter of my wrist and at least
one foot long. I then split this piece in half and let it
dry on a south-facing window sill for at least a week.
Splitting the branch allows for a faster drying time.

> SPECIFIC TREE SPECIES

As mentioned earlier, soft woods make ideal bow drill kits.
Below is a list of trees in order of my preference for both
the spindle and hearth board. Where applicable I also list
other noteworthy facts about these incredible survival
resources.

>> Basswood (American Linden)

Besides balsa, I know of no softer wood than basswood.
Also known as the American Linden, basswood is a
favorite of wood carvers. My friends from the UK
refer to this tree as Lime. Except for areas of extreme
climates, basswood can be found in most of the northern hemisphere. It is a water lover and will almost
always be found growing around water.

Basswood leaves are somewhat heart shaped and almost always asymmetrical. They have a small, pea-shaped fruit that dangles from a tongue-shaped bract. Young, tender basswood leaves are among my favorite wild edible greens. I make basswood salads several times a week in early spring.

The "bass" in basswood comes from the word "bast," which means fiber. The inner-bark fibers of the basswood tree make incredible natural cordage. Instant basswood bark cordage can easily be obtained in spring and summer months by peeling the bark from younger suckers or saplings. You will find this cordage to be flexible and strong. I have made many a bow drill string using basswood cordage. The bark from slightly older basswood trees (3 – 5 inches in diameter) can be pounded and peeled from the trunk during the same time of year when the sap is flowing heavy. After soaking in water for 3 – 4 weeks (called "retting") the inner bark fibers will easily peel away from the rough exterior bark in long, ribbon-like sheets.

I recall one summer when lightning struck a large basswood tree at the edge of the pond near my training facility. This powerful strike caused the bark of that large tree to be blown from the trunk in several massive sheets, around 2 feet wide and 20 feet long. After soaking them in the pond I was able to gather several wheelbarrows of basswood cordage, which I used in training for many years after.

While I've used basswood of every age and type for bow drill kits, my favorite is that which is sourced from sucker trees that are 2 – 4 inches in diameter. The consistency of fast-growing sucker wood is unlike wood cut from the main tree. However, green sucker wood will require drying time. If you find a standing sucker tree that's already dead, count yourself lucky. If suckers are not available, low-hanging branches are a good second choice.

Cottonwood Leaf

>>Cottonwood

Cottonwoods were a favorite among Native Americans across North America, as the trees were used to make dugout canoes. (*Often, these were coal burned.*) Cottonwood trees have a triangular-shaped leaf with toothed edges. The bark is deeply fissured. Like basswoods, cottonwoods grow primarily around water. I've seen massive cottonwoods along streams from Arizona to Virginia.

Cottonwoods grow very fast—almost too fast for their own good. The combination of this fast growth and their soft wood makes for very weak branches, which is a good thing when searching for stock to make your spindle and hearth board. Dead, broken branches can almost always be found littering the base of large cottonwoods and hung up in smaller trees or underbrush nearby.

Cottonwood Seedpod

During the spring, when the cottonwood bears the source of its name, one can gather not only wood for the spindle and hearth boards, but tinder bundles as well. Cottonwoods produce seeds that are covered in cotton-like down. When gathered together, these downy clusters make a very flammable tinder bundle.

>>Eastern White Cedar

The eastern white cedar grows primarily in the northern woods of the United States and into Canada, but I've had success with many different cedar varieties including western red cedar from the Pacific Northwest. Cedars are coniferous evergreens and are easily identified by their flat, fan-like branches with scaly leaves.

The dead lower branches (also known as "squaw wood") often make excellent spindle and hearth board choices. Shredded cedar bark makes one of the most effective tinder bundles.

It can easily be processed by scraping a knife at a 90-degree angle against the tree. The bark will shred off in fibrous masses that can be further processed by rubbing the shredded bark between the palms of your hands until they reach a hair-like consistency.

>> Alder

There are several species of alders that are native to North America, including sitka, red, white and thin leaf. Although not an evergreen, the dead giveaway of a female alder is its tiny wooden cones ("strobili") that you'll find on the branch tips throughout winter. Male alders have longer, softer catkins that hang down like little caterpillars. The leaves are egg shaped and serrated.

Like most trees that work best for making friction f ires, alders grow near water. Red alder is considered a favorite for bow drills in the Pacific Northwest, but the tree grows almost everywhere in North America, excluding extreme environments.

>> Sycamore

The sycamore tree, another water lover, is nearly impossible to misidentify. Its very unique bark has a winter camouflage effect: mottled with whites, tans, creams and grays. As the tree grows, the exterior bark peels off to the ground in thin, brown curls, leaving a pure white base layer exposed. No other tree in the forest has bark that looks like or behaves like the sycamore's. When layered into a large cigar-style roll, a thick tube of sycamore bark also makes for an excellent fire carry. It will smolder a red hot ember, which can be used to blow a tinder bundle into flame when desired.

The sycamore tree also produces small balls of clustered seeds in the fall, which can be broken apart and incorporated into a tinder bundle. The seed clusters alone don't make an ideal tinder bundle, but they are great filler when mixed with dried grasses, pine needles or bark fibers.

Like the cottonwood, the base of all sycamores will be littered with dead and broken branches all year round. These branches make very serviceable spindles and hearth boards. Sycamores also grow suckers at the base, which can be used.

Other noteworthy bow drill trees are:
- Willow
- Staghorn Sumac
- Aspen
- Tulip Poplar

My first successful bow drill kit wasn't made from a tree at all, but from a woody, stalked plant – the yucca. In fact, there are several noteworthy plants with woody stalks that make fantastic bow drill spindles and hearth boards. Some of the fastest embers I've seen generated with a bow drill were from those carved from woody, stalked plants. Let's discuss a few of the most popular of these.

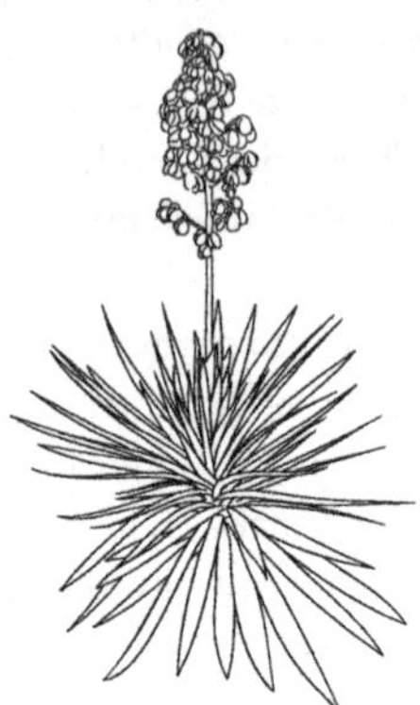

>> Yucca

I list yucca first because it has a special place in my heart since it was the first material I learned to use in my bow drill kit. It makes an excellent choice for first-time drillers. Yucca is a plant native to America's Southwest, not to be confused with yuca, also known as manioc or cassava, which has an edible root. Yucca is a popular ornamental plant and can now be found all over the United States and throughout the world. It grows in arid deserts as well as the four-season eastern woodlands. Even the harshest of winters will not kill it. I've often found it growing in old cemeteries, where it no doubt was planted as an ornamental.

The leaves of the yucca are green and sword-like. Beware of the very sharp points on the tips. They grow from a central rosette and remain green year-round. There are many different species of yucca (some even growing into large yucca trees). While not edible, the yucca root is loaded with saponins and can be crushed and used as soap for washing.

Yucca's claim to fame is its fibrous leaves, which are filled with long, strong fibers that can be woven into durable survival cordage. (This process is covered in great detail in my Pocket Field Guide entitled *NATURAL CORDAGE.*) Immediate cordage can be sourced from the green leaves, but I prefer to use the dead leaves that typically can be found around the base of the plant. It is very easy to slough off the brown, flaky exterior and extract the fibers from the already-dead, dried leaves. I have successfully used yucca leaf cordage combined with a yucca stalk spindle and hearth board for many bow drill kits. Yucca is nearly a one-stop shop when it comes to gathering bow drill kit components.

The stalk of the yucca grows from the center of the plant starting in early spring. The height and diameter it reaches depends upon the species and age of the plant. Beautiful white flowers (which are actually edible) bloom all around the stalk, creating a very impressive display in spring and summer. Soon after full bloom, the yucca stalk begins to die, dry, and harden. By late fall and all through the winter it's ready to be cut off at the base and used for a bow drill spindle and hearth board. The lightweight, porous consistency of this dead, dry, woody stalk makes for one of the best bow drill spindles available on earth. The trick can sometimes be finding a stalk that is thick enough AND straight enough to be used as a drill and hearth.

>> Sotol

Sotol, also known as desert spoon, is similar in appearance to yucca. It, too, is an evergreen and produces long, thin, sword-shaped leaves in a circular pattern around the base. Unlike yucca, sotol cannot handle prolonged cold and therefore grows exclusively in the warm, arid environments of America's Southwest, including the Sonoran Desert of Arizona.

Like the yucca, sotol produces a central flower stalk that is adorned with a bristle-like plume of tiny white flowers. This stalk can grow as tall as 20 feet, and I've seen them as large as 2 – 3 inches in diameter. The leaf edges are lined with sharp, barbed thorns, so use caution when cutting the stalk from the base.

The dead, dry, and woody stalk is used extensively for the fire plow method of friction fire-starting and is large enough to make many bow drill kits. This stalk works incredibly well for bow drill and is highly recommended if you reside in an area where the sotol plant is native.

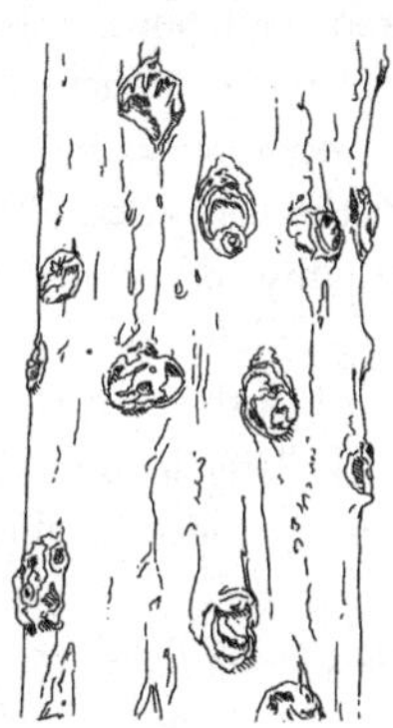

>> **Elderberry** (*Sambucus*)

Elderberry is a deciduous shrub found throughout the Northern Hemisphere, except in areas with extreme climates. A year-round identifying feature of the elderberry it its bark. The exterior of the bark is covered with evenly spaced little raised "bark warts." This is a very unique feature of the elderberry.

In spring, the elderberry bush produces flat, dinner-plate-sized flowers, which are actually made up of many small white flowers. These flowers can be battered and fried (elderberry fritters), but they are traditionally used to make elderberry syrup after being steeped in sugar water. If left to their own devices, the flowers will ultimately transform into clusters of berries colored from purple to black. These are used to make jellies, jams, wines, and all sorts of other delicious treats. All other parts of elderberry are poisonous.

The elderberry branch is unique in that it has a very large pith with a Styrofoam consistency. It's one of the very few bushes/trees/woody, stalked plants that can be hollowed out. It's the soft wood of the elderberry combined with its pithy center that makes it a wonderful bow drill spindle candidate. An elderberry spindle is better paired with a hearth board made from a different type of wood. It's challenging to create a proper hearth from an elderberry stalk because of its central pith.

*Special Note: Because of the pithy center, it can be difficult to carve the top of the spindle to a point. Consequently, it is better left rounded.

First Year Mullein

>> Mullein

The dead, dry stalk of the mullein plant in fall and winter makes a very suitable bow drill spindle. Much like elderberry, it is better paired with a hearth board made from a different wood because a suitable hearth board is difficult to split out from a pithy-centered mullein stalk.

Mullein, also known as lamb's ear, has large, pale-green, fuzz-covered leaves in spring and summer. The plant has a two-year life cycle. The first year it grows a low rosette of large fuzzy leaves that are nature's perfect toilet paper and padded inserts for shoes. During its second year it shoots up a tall, straight, and woody stalk topped with masses of beautiful little yellow flowers. This stalk is almost always perfectly straight and I've started many a bow drill fire with a mullein spindle.

The woody stalk is firm, yet soft, and the center is filled with a dense pith. One fall I built an entire bow drill kit (excluding the bow string) from one giant mullein. I used the root for the bearing block; the stalk for the spindle, hearth and bow; and the leaves and seed head for the tinder bundle.

Second Year Mullein

***Special Note:** *Because of the pithy center, it can be difficult to carve the top of the spindle to a point. Consequently, it is better left rounded.*

NOTES:

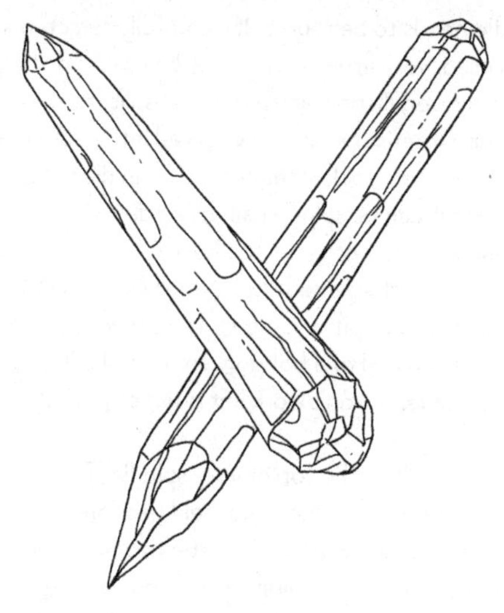

SPINDLE
CARVING INSTRUCTIONS & DETAILS

Now that many different tree and plant options have been covered for harvesting the spindle and hearth board, let's discuss the details of making these components. We'll start first with the spindle.

In my experience, the best length for a bow drill spindle is 8 – 10 inches. The diameter should be similar to that of your thumb, roughly half an inch to an inch wide. It should also be straight and free of knots, cracks, bark, and forks.

The spindle needs to be round. If a carefully selected straight branch is used, very little carving may be required along the length. However, if the spindle must be split from a larger piece of stock then it must be carefully carved into a round, dowel shape. If a piece of stock at least 2 inches in diameter can be sourced then it can be split in half; one side will serve as the spindle blank and the other as the hearth board. One end of the spindle should be sharpened like a pencil (this won't be possible with stock that has a pithy center). The other end should be rounded, like the end of a hot dog. Try to make it as perfectly round as possible. It won't work if it is flat or jagged in any way.

The sharp end will be the top of your spindle. This is where pressure is applied from the hand-held bearing block. The top is sharpened because you want as little friction as possible. The least amount of wood spinning against the bearing block, the better. The rounded end is the business end of your spindle. It moves against your hearth board, where you want as much friction and surface area on the board as possible to increase heat.

Don't make the mistake of meticulously carving the sides (length-wise) of your spindle to be perfectly smooth. A roughly carved surface will provide necessary traction for the bow string. I've had to "roughen-up" many a student's spindle with fresh cuts along the length to prevent string slippage while drilling.

Finally, the spindle should have as even a diameter from top to bottom as possible. If it tapers in either direction the bow string will likely follow that taper, making it more difficult for a beginner.

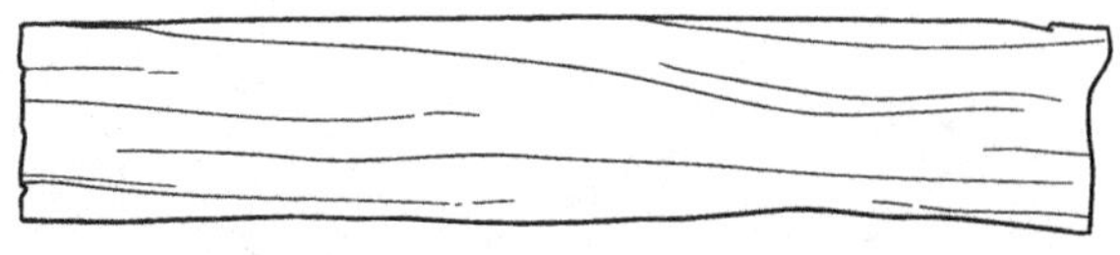

HEARTHBOARD
CARVING INSTRUCTIONS & DETAILS

Like the spindle, the hearth should also be straight and free
of knots, cracks, bark, and forks. Hearth boards perform
best with soft woods that are between half an inch and
three-quarters of an inch thick. The length of the hearth
board can vary greatly, but around 12 inches is ideal. The
ideal width of a hearth board is 2 inches or greater, although
I've used boards many times that are about the same width
as the diameter of the spindle. The hearth must be flat on
both sides so it can rest securely under one's foot and on
the ground. A hearth board that is not flat may rock or twist
while you drill, which is a common rookie mistake.

The most controlled method for splitting out a hearth board from a larger piece of stock is to cut the stock to length first—approximately 12 inches. Then your knife can be batoned lengthwise through the stock using a solid stick (called a baton) about 2 inches in diameter. Batoning allows for very precise and calculated splits to be made. Your knife should be placed at a 90-degree angle, blade down, on top of the upright stock. You will then strike the spine of your knife with the baton, driving it downward like a sharp wedge and splitting the stock to your desired width. If using a round branch for the hearth, both sides will need to be batoned in order to make it flat on top and bottom.

> STORE-BOUGHT SPINDLE & HEARTH TRAINING KIT

For the purposes of practice and training, you can buy kiln-dried rough cedar trim boards from the hardware store. A single 1 inch x 2 inch x 8 foot trim board can supply many spindle and hearth kits. This is what I use when teaching bow drill training courses. You will need two 10 inch sections to make your spindle and hearth board. One 10 inch section is the completed hearth with no further modifications. Split the second 10 inch section lengthwise to yield two equal spindle blanks and then round them out. I have had wonderful success with this store-bought cedar material. For your convenience, here are the trim board item numbers from two popular home improvement stores that carry this stock.

LOWES Home Improvement Store Item #:
7592 (Cedar Board Reversible Rough/Smooth)

HOME DEPOT Store Item #:
500-541 (7/8x2x8 KD Cedar Board)

I also sell ready-made Bow Drill Kits that have been tested and proven to work on my web-site at www.creekstewart.com.

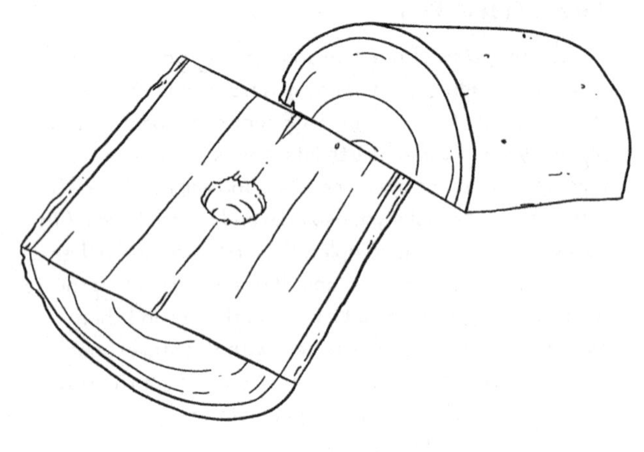

BEARING BLOCK

> DESCRIPTION & FUNCTION

The bearing block is held in the palm of the driller's non-dominant hand to provide downward pressure on the spindle as it spins into the hearth board. Since you want the friction to occur in the hearth board and not the bearing block, measures must be taken to reduce friction between the pointed spindle top and the recessed divot on the underside of the bearing block where the spindle top fits.

> WOOD PROPERTIES & SELECTION

An ideal bow drill bearing block is cut from a round of very hard (and preferably live) green wood. Remember, you want the top of the spindle to rotate with as little of friction as possible in the bearing block divot. A soft, dry bearing block will only cause the top of the spindle to heat up and smoke at the point of contact. The bearing block has no reason to be dry or soft. In fact, it performs best when wet, slick and hard.

> CARVING INSTRUCTIONS & DETAILS

The bearing block is very simple to carve. First, cut a 4-inch section of a live, green branch or sapling that is approximately 2 inches in diameter.

A QUICK CONSERVATION NOTE:

Be sure to be selective when cutting a branch or tree for use as a bearing block. Look at this act as pruning the forest. If a branch or sucker sapling is selectively chosen because of a defect or overcrowding, pruning it from the tree or forest can actually be beneficial. Use caution and don't haphazardly cut a live bearing block from a healthy tree in a healthy location simply because it's convenient. Look for a suitable bearing block from a tree or branch that will benefit from a selective pruning.

Once a 4"x2" section of hard, green wood has been secured, it should be batoned in half to make 2 equal half-rounds. One of these half-rounds will serve as the bearing block blank.

A simple twisting of the knife point into the center flat bottom of the half-round will create a small, funnel-shaped divot. An average bearing block divot should be approximately one-quarter-inch deep. This will be the seat for the top of the bow drill spindle.

Care should be taken to make sure the top, rounded portion of the bearing block is carved smooth because that is where you will be holding it. You want it to be free of any rough places that may result in hot spots on the palm of your hand while using the kit.

> BEARING BLOCK TIPS & TRICKS

Any effort that reduces friction between the bearing block and spindle will yield rewards in terms of both time and energy once drilling begins. Below are several bearing block/spindle modification tips and tricks I've found useful over the years.

- Crush pencil lead (graphite) and coat the bearing block divot with it to reduce friction.

- Smash and rub green leaves into the bearing block divot to create a slick, damp, gooey surface. I've found that mucilaginous plants such as jewelweed, basswood leaves, aloe and cattail work the best.

- Dip the top of the spindle in grease, water, wax, petroleum, lip balm, or any similar lubricant before drilling.

>> Wood Alternative Bearing Blocks

Some of the best bearing blocks I've used haven't even

been wood. My favorite is a wooden half-round into which I fitted a skateboard wheel bearing (drilling a hole to secure it there). This provides a nearly frictionless bearing block as the spindle rotates in the wheel bearing. Stone bearing blocks were quite common in primitive cultures. Divots in stone can now be drilled with modern tools, but our ancestors chipped and pecked them out with harder rocks such as chert, quartz, and flint. Some of my favorite artifact finds have been smooth, palm-sized stones with a small divot on one side that I believe must have once been primitive bearing blocks. A dedicated search in rocky streambeds or cliffs can often yield a suitable rock with a naturally worn divot that does not need altered.

Bone and antler make excellent bearing blocks as well. They are both very dense and the divot can be polished as smooth as glass. Unlike their wooden counterparts, bone and antler do not wear away so they will last indefinitely.

Countless modern implements can also be used as makeshift bearing blocks, including shot glasses, spoons, ladles, plastic pieces, and chunks of metal. When pounded with a ball-peen hammer into a small bowl shape and glued into a carved depression, copper pennies and beer-bottle caps make excellent, low-friction bearing block divot liners. Divots can also be coated with a variety of hard-sealing epoxies for a smooth surface. Coming up with wood-alternative bearing blocks is a great way to inspire your resourcefulness and creativity.

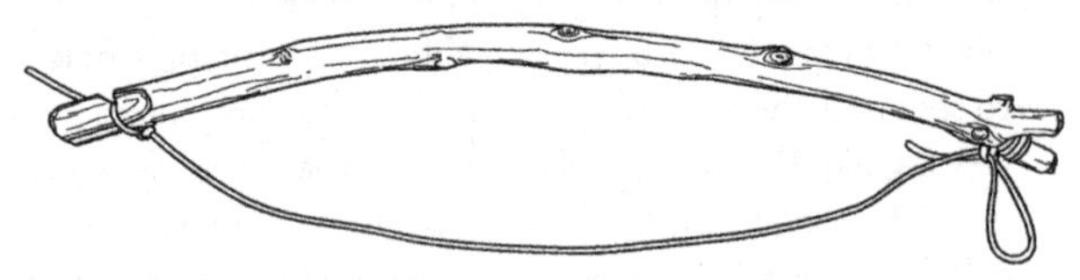

THE BOW

> DESCRIPTION & FUNCTION

The bow, when fitted with a bow string, allows you to rotate the spindle. When the spindle is wrapped on the bow string, a pushing and pulling of the bow causes the spindle to turn with impressive velocity, creating the friction you need to get a hot, glowing ember. The bow offers a mechanical advantage for rotating the spindle much faster than if you were to rub the spindle between your hands, and it takes a lot less energy.

> WOOD PROPERTIES & SELECTION

The bow should be approximately the length of your fingertip to armpit. It should be cut from either green or seasoned wood approximately 1-inch in diameter. Look for wood that is very sturdy and solid. Many people assume it should be flexible, like the kind of bow you use to shoot an arrow, but that is not true. You actually don't want the wood to flex at all. I prefer a bow that has a slight curve to it, similar to the shape of a parenthesis "(". I've also used

nearly straight bows on many occasions, but first-time
success rates seem to be a little higher with curved bows.

Like most of the other bow drill components, the bow
should be free of knots, branches and cracks.

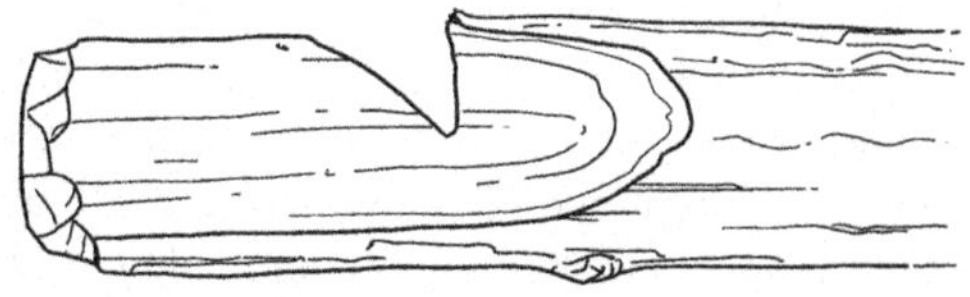

> CARVING INSTRUCTIONS & DETAILS

A functional bow shouldn't require much knife work. At
most, two string notches will need to be carved. A carefully selected bow with a small y-fork at top will eliminate
the need to carve one of them.

There are many different ways to carve a string notch. I
recommend a number-7 notch. As can be seen in the
illustration above, the notch on the end of the bow
resembles a number 7 on the outside edge. This notch style
provides a very secure anchor point for the bow string.
Carving the notches is made easier by first thinning the
sides of each end to give it a flatter profile.

A very simple and efficient technique for carving a number-7
notch is to first make a quarter-inch saw cut with a pocket
folding saw or multi-tool. The notch is then quickly
finished with several push cuts with a knife to form the
number-7 profile. This process takes a few seconds.

Many different varieties of cordage, both man-made and natural, can serve as the bow string. For training, teaching and practice, I prefer to use 550 parachute cord, also called paracord. Paracord is an incredible multifunction survival cord. It has a tensile strength of 550 pounds and also has seven inner strands that can be pulled out and used for fishing line, gear repair and an infinite number of other functions. I have replaced all of my shoelaces with 550 paracord so that I have it on my person at all times. A woven paracord survival bracelet is another convenient way to carry 550 cord.

I always tell my students that if they can tie their shoes they can secure a bow drill string. I use the same knot on both ends. It's called a double half hitch. It's simply an overhand knot followed by a half hitch. It's easy to tie and easy to untie, both of which are important when quick adjustments need to be made to tighten or loosen the string around the spindle. See the illustration below for tying details.

Although you will likely have to adjust the tautness of the bow drill string at least once during the drill process, I start by tying the first double half hitch on one end and then pull the string taught to the other end. I then give the string approximately 1-inch of slack and tie off the other end with the second double half hitch. This is typically about the right amount of slack to wrap the average-size spindle. (*More details about wrapping the spindle will be given later.*)

NOTES:

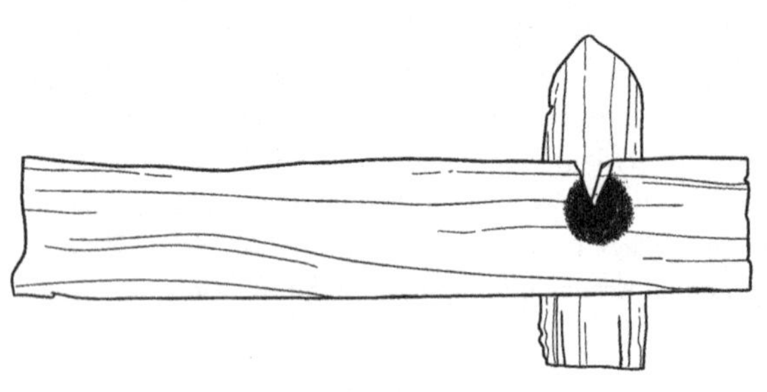

EMBER CATCH

> DESCRIPTION & FUNCTION

The ember catch, also called the ember pan, is a small, flat pan made from one of a huge variety of materials. You must place it beneath the notch in the hearth board so it can catch the bow drill ember you will eventually create as you drill. The ember catch prevents the ember from falling onto the ground and from wicking up ground moisture that may exist under the hearth board. The ember catch also allows you to pick the ember up and transfer it into your tinder bundle.

The ember catch can be almost anything that is dry and flat enough to fit flush between the hearth board and the ground. Other than being durable enough to withstand the heat from a smoldering ember, it does not have to be made from a special material. It should be around the size of a standard business card.

Below is a list of potential ember catches:

• Wood shaving from carving your spindle or hearth board

• Thin piece of metal such as one cut from an empty soda can

• Small piece of leather

• Several dry leaves sandwiched together

• Thin strip of bark

• Piece of cardboard

• Several pieces of paper sandwiched together

COMPONENT:

TINDER BUNDLE

> DESCRIPTION & FUNCTION

The tinder bundle is a prepared nest of fibrous and dry materials. It is the material that burns when a bow drill ember is blown into flame. The bow drill ember is placed in the tinder bundle and then you blow on the ember and bring about an open flame. The tinder bundle allows you to make the leap from smoldering ember to open flame.

I've seen too many students labor for a bow drill ember only for it to be wasted on a poorly chosen or constructed tinder bundle. Making fire with a bow drill kit comes down to the tinder bundle. It needs to be sourced and built ahead of time. You can spin out the largest ember ever created, but if you dump it into a poorly chosen tinder bundle you will not get flames. A bow drill succeeds when open flame is achieved. It is ultimately open flame that will facilitate survival, not a fragile smoldering bow drill ember.

I prefer large tinder bundles that are similar in size to an average cantaloupe—around 8 – 10 inches in diameter. The first rule is that a tinder bundle must be made from dry material. Nothing alive is dry enough. The tinder must be dead and dry. Two large handfuls should be enough. The tinder chosen should be fibrous in consistency. Dry grasses, bark fibers, some leaves, dead seed pods and plant fibers are all good choices.

A tinder bundle consists of two main parts: the body and the core. The body comprises the bulk of the tinder bundle. The core is the center of the tinder bundle where the ember will ultimately be placed. To make the core, select your best tinder—the driest, most fibrous material that you can find. You want to give your ember the best chance of success. On the following page are good tinder options for the body and core:

BODY TINDER SUGGESTIONS

- Dry grasses that have been twisted and rubbed between the hands to increase fibrous qualities and expose plant fibers

- Cedar bark that has been "bushed" between your palms and processed into a fibrous ball

- Tulip popular bark that has been "bushed" between the palms and processed into a fibrous ball

- Palm tree fibers

- Dried and dead yucca, agave, and sotol leaves that have been twisted and rubbed between your hands to increase fibrous qualities and expose leaf fibers

- Pine needles (*not the best option, but they do work*)

- Clematis bark that has been peeled and "bushed" to increase fibrous qualities

- Shredded newspaper (*urban tinder*)

- Shredded cotton rags or clothing (*urban tinder*)

- Cotton balls, tampons, and cotton face wipes (*urban tinder*)

CORE TINDER SUGGESTIONS

- Dry, fluffy seed pods
- Cattail seed down
- Milkweed seed down
- Extremely well-processed cedar bark
- Dried sage leaves
- Dried sweetgrass leaves
- Dried tobacco (*cigarette tobacco—urban tinder*)
- Cotton balls (*urban tinder*)
- Dryer lint (*urban tinder*)

> TINDER BUNDLE CONSTRUCTION & DETAILS

Imagine a cross between a football and a bird's nest. This is what a well-constructed tinder bundle should look like. It should be football-shaped with a small depression in the middle about the size of a golf ball.

The football portion should be made from the body tinder materials. Then press a palm-sized wad of core tinder into the golf-ball-sized cavity. It is here where the ember will be placed so it can easily ignite the most flammable materials and become an open flame.

The tinder bundle should always be prepared in advance of spinning out a bow drill ember. Keep it close at hand, at the ready.

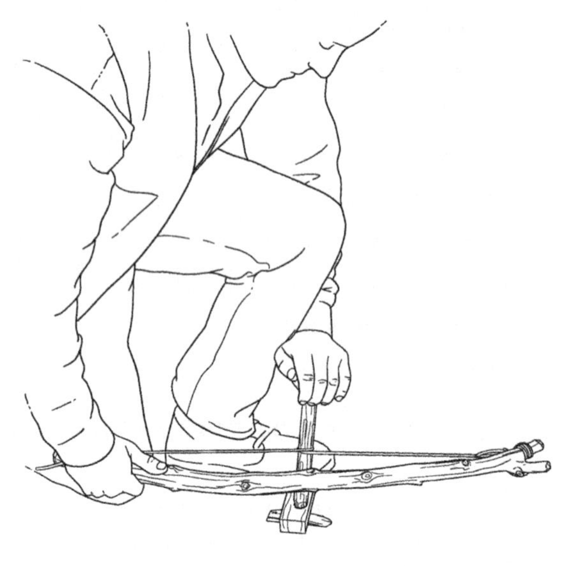

BOW DRILL
FORM, TECHNIQUE & PROCESS

Once all of the components are collected, processed, carved, and prepared, it's time to assemble your fire-making kit. The following steps are right-handed instructions. For left-handed drillers, simply switch the words RIGHT and LEFT from here forward.

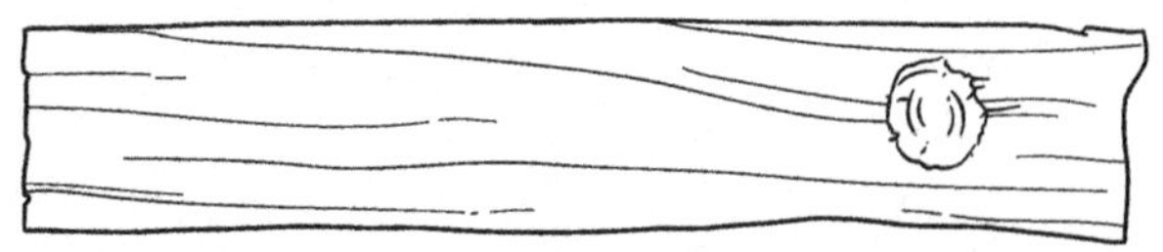

>> Step 1: Carve the Seat Divot

Before you start rotating the spindle you will need to carve a small, rounded depression in the hearth board. This is where the rounded end (bottom) of the spindle will sit. Without a seat divot it's extremely challenging if not impossible to keep the spindle turning in one place when drilling begins.

The seat divot should be carved approximately 2 inches in from the right side of the hearth board and 1-inch back from the front edge, as shown in the illustration. It should be at most a quarter-inch deep and close to the same diameter as the bottom of the spindle.

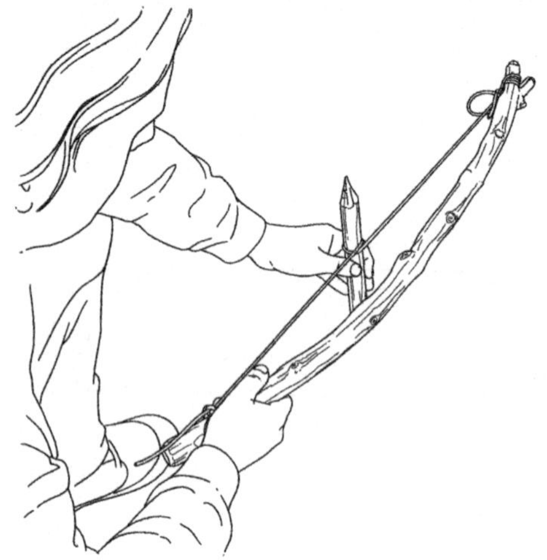

>> Step 2: Wrap the Spindle in the Bow String

This can be the most difficult part of mastering the bow drill. With the bow in your right hand (bow facing right, string facing left) and the spindle in your left hand, twist the spindle into the bow string so that the string wraps around the spindle one time. The sharp end of the spindle (top) should be facing upward and the spindle should be positioned on the OUTSIDE of the string as opposed to on the INSIDE of the string. See illustration above for details.

I'm always asked how to wrap the spindle and my reply is always "Just try it. If it isn't right, unwrap it and try again!" The best way to learn is to experiment until you get it right. It's hard to learn this from a written explanation, but here are the basic instructions.

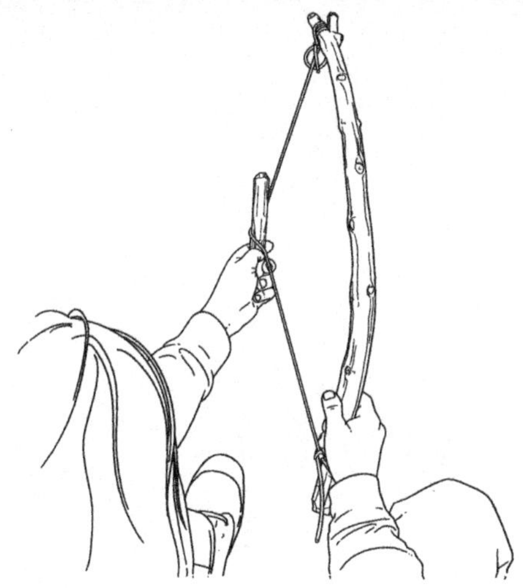

Hold the strung bow and spindle parallel to the ground.
Now bring the rounded (bottom) end of the spindle
under the bow string. Then bring it up and over the
string while pushing the top of the spindle forward so
that it causes the bow string to twist around the spindle.
The string should be wrapped around the spindle and the
spindle should be straight up and down on the outside of
the string.

The string should be very tight around the spindle. You
should not be able to slide the spindle up or down the
bow string if it is wrapped correctly. The spindle should
be able to only rotate along the string, and it should not
slip or slide. Adjustments in the bow string may need to
be made at this point if the spindle is too loose or if the
string is so tight that the spindle can't be wrapped.

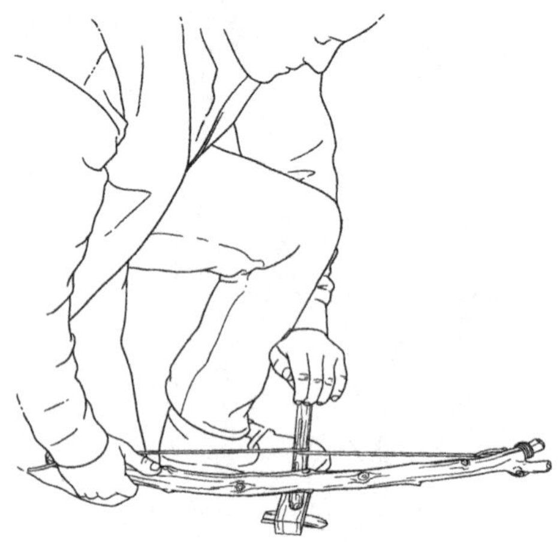

>> Step 3: Burn in the Seat

Now you are ready to spin the spindle against the hearth board, but your goal in this step is not to achieve an ember. You are simply burning in a better seat in the small divot that you carved in Step 1.

With your spindle wrapped and your hearth board on flat, solid ground in front of you, place your left foot on the hearth board and crouch down. Put your right knee on the ground. The carved divot on the hearth board should be on your right side and facing away from you.

Now pick up the bearing block in your left hand. Your left hand will come around in front of your left knee and shin and the bearing block will be used to apply downward pressure on the wrapped spindle, holding it securely into the carved seat on the hearth board.

CRITICAL NOTE: *Before and during spindle rotation, your left wrist must be braced against your left shin to stabilize it. I can't emphasize this enough. Not stabilizing the left wrist and bearing block is the most common reason for failure at the bow drill.*

Once your left wrist is braced against the front of your left shin, grab the very back of the bow with your right hand and start to slowly rotate the spindle by pushing the bow forward and pulling it backward. Don't go too fast at first—just fast enough to get a rhythm. Concentrate on form and keeping the spindle in the carved divot seat. Make sure you're comfortable and don't forget to breath! BRACE THAT WRIST!

As you feel more comfortable, increase speed with the bow. Be sure to utilize the entire length of the bow string, drawing it all the way to the front and all the way to the back. The bow is your mechanical advantage. USE IT. As you increase bow speed, apply slightly more pressure on the bearing block.

If you've chosen your materials properly you will start to smell and see smoke within 10 – 15 passes of the bow. You'll also notice a change in feel and sound as your spindle begins to char and burn the divot in your hearth board. Once your kit starts to smoke, continue for 5 more passes and then stop.

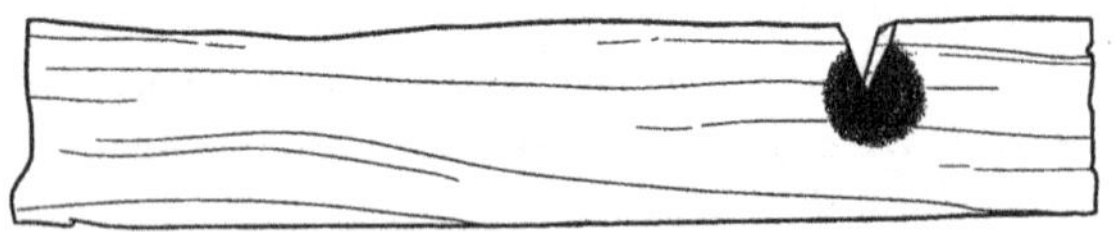

>> Step 4: Carve the Hearth Board Notch

As the spindle rotates against the hearth board it creates a fine, charred dust. You'll see it at this point in the process if you look closely. When you're trying to achieve an ember, this dust will ultimately become your ember as the temperature increases enough to ignite it into a smolder. At this point you need to create an area on the hearth board to collect and contain this charred wood dust. You can do this by carving a pie-shaped notch into the center of the freshly charred hearth board spindle seat.

The notch should be approximately an eighth of the entire charred seat divot. The tip of the notch should extend to the exact middle of the charred circle. It should be cut all the way through the hearth board and should be cleared of shavings, splinters, or any debris that would interfere with char dust collection.

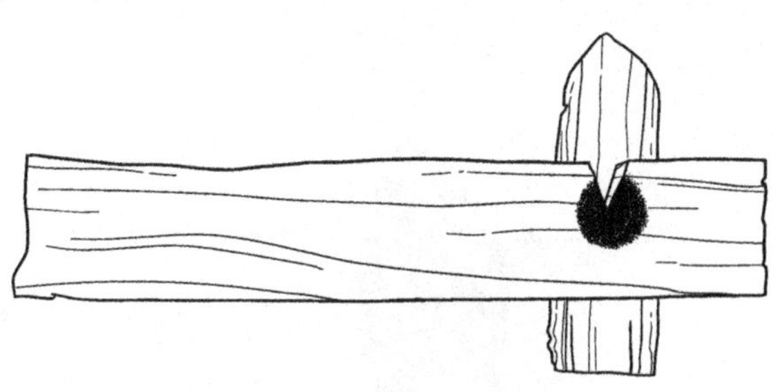

>> Step 5: Place Ember Catch and Reset Kit

Now that the notch is carved, it's important to place your ember catch under it before going for ember. Do this now. Before drilling again, take a minute to touch up your kit if necessary and make sure your bow string is still at the desired tautness.

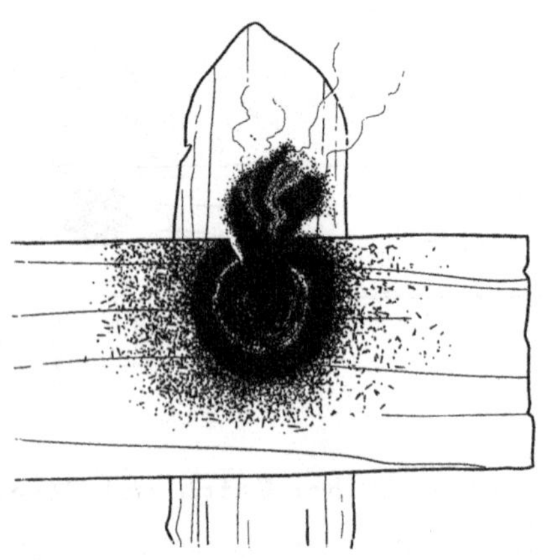

>> Step 6: Go for Ember

With a proper charred seat burned in and the ember catch in place, it's now time to go for an ember. Reset as before. Don't forget to brace that wrist! Also, you need to have a tinder bundle at the ready before proceeding. Follow the steps below:

- Position the kit; spindle in bearing block and on hearth board. Left wrist should be braced against front of left shin.

- Start to push and pull the bow, slowly at first to build a rhythm.

- Utilize the full bow, drawing it all the way to front, all the way to back.

- Begin to speed up. After 10-15 passes the kit will start to smoke like before. You should start to see a little dust begin to collect in the notch.

- When your kit starts to smoke, push and pull the bow faster and apply a little more downward pressure with the bearing block. Be sure to keep the bow PARALLEL with the ground so the bow string doesn't ride up or down the spindle. Continue for 10-15 more passes.

- IF ANYTHING DOESN'T FEEL RIGHT, STOP, ADJUST AND RESET.

- By now, you should see quite a bit of dust collecting in your notch. It should be light-to-dark brown in color. You need it to be dark-brown-to-black in color.

- Now, for 5 – 8 seconds, push and pull as fast as you can, giving it all you have, while maintaining steady downward pressure with the bearing block. You will see dust pouring into the notch and darkening in color. Then slowly stop and remove the spindle.

EXPERT FIELD TIP

The color of bow drill dust tells the user a lot! If the dust color is light brown or coffee colored and you have not achieved an ember, then you will need to increase drilling speed and pressure. The ideal dust color shouldbe very dark brown to black. If the dust is black and crusty and no ember is achieved, it is likely that too much pressure has been applied.

Fire requires heat, fuel, and oxygen to thrive. If there is an ember within the dust in your notch, it will need oxygen to stay alive. Gently fan it with your hand to give it a little bit of oxygen. The notch should be filled with dust, hopefully smoking on its own.

Gently take your knife tip, a blade of grass, a wood shaving or a small twig and release the ember dust from the notch by carefully pushing it while pulling away the hearth board. Sometimes, tapping the hearth board will free the ember from the notch as well. If you have an ember, it will continue to smoke on its own.

If it is not smoking on its own, adjust your kit, reset and retry.

If it is smoking on its own then continue to fan it gently with your hand and wait for the red ember to grow through to the top of the small pile of dust. Protect it from the wind, rain or snow.

>> Step 7: Grow Your Ember

You've worked very hard to get an ember. Don't let impatience screw it up now. Take a few minutes and grow your ember. Sure, you can take that tiny little ember and place it into a tinder bundle and blow it into flame, but when it comes to bow drill embers, BIGGER IS ALWAYS BETTER! I've seen more students than I'd like to admit lose a tiny, fragile ember after all their hard work, and it could have been prevented if they'd taken a few minutes to grow it.

One of the best-kept bow drill secrets for quickly and easily growing a bow drill ember is PUNKY WOOD. Punky wood is dry, semi-rotted wood that can easily be powdered between the fingertips. You've walked by and stepped over punky wood many times and probably didn't even notice. Almost every dead, broken branch turns to punky wood eventually. Decaying stumps almost always go through a punky wood phase and hollow trees are full of it. It must be dry and you must be able to powder it by pinching and rubbing it between your fingertips.

Once you've tapped your ember out of the ember notch and let the red ember grow through to the top, slowly sprinkle punky wood powder on top of it. The ember will grow as it consumes the punky wood. The more punky wood you add, the larger (and more stable) the ember grows. I suggest growing it to the diameter of a quarter before placing it in your tinder bundle.

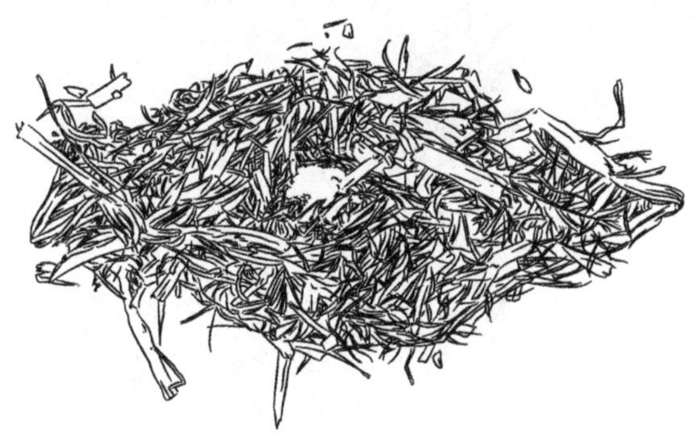

>> Step 8: Place Ember in Tinder Bundle

Although the ember can be transported using the ember catch, it's important to bring the tinder bundle to the ember. The ember is still fragile and vulnerable to movement and wind. Set the prepared tinder bundle right next to the ember and gently dump the ember from the ember catch into the tinder bundle core. If your ember is a proper size, as discussed earlier, there is no need to hurry. Sometimes it may be necessary to tap the ember catch to release the ember, or you may need to scrape it off with a knife blade.

Once in the tinder bundle core, it's extremely important to envelop the ember in the tinder bundle by folding the edges of the tinder bundle over the top. Don't crush it; just envelop it. A main function of the tinder bundle is to contain the heat from the ember as it grows through the fibers. This is best accomplished when the ember is protected and enveloped by the tinder bundle.

>> Step 9: Blow into Flame

Now your ember will need oxygen in order to grow and eventually ignite the tinder bundle. This is accomplished by steady, even breaths gently blown into the core. If there is a natural wind blowing, position your body so that your back is to the wind so the smoke from the tinder bundle isn't blown into your face, which complicates the process with coughing and watery eyes. Remember that smoke rises, so position the tinder bundle at an angle above the face rather than blowing down on it. Sometimes, a natural wind will provide the oxygen necessary to achieve open flame.

Stubborn tinder bundles can take quite an effort to blow into flame. If a break is needed from blowing, the tinder bundle can be gently waved in a sweeping motion back and forth to provide an influx of oxygen. This strategy can be very effective.

As a general rule, the more your tinder bundle smokes, the more oxygen it needs. The more smoke you see, the harder you can blow. If the tinder material was carefully chosen and the bundle was packed tightly enough to contain the heat from the growing ember, then open flame should be less than a minute or two away!

Fire likes to climb. Once open flame is achieved, the tinder bundle should be rotated upside down and placed into a prepared fire lay of larger kindling materials. The open flame will then climb up through the tinder bundle and ignite your larger kindling.

CONCLUSION

In my experience, once a student has tried and failed at the bow drill three times in a row, the success rate drops significantly. If you try for an ember three times and don't get it, take a break and try again after you've had time to rest, catch your breath and decompress. During that time, reevaluate your kit or carve a new one. Then give it another shot.

I consider the ability to make fire from sticks one of my greatest life accomplishments. It has taught me much about fire principles and my own personal capabilities and limitations. I hope you, too, will add the bow drill to your list of survival skill sets. I also hope that the bow drill is just the beginning in your friction-fire adventures.

If you like this guide, check out my other Pocket Field Guides at **www.creekstewart.com.**

Share your success with this skill on social media using **#creekstewart** & **#pocketfieldguide**

Remember, it's not IF *but* WHEN,
CREEK

NOTES:

NOTES:

NOTES:

NOTES:

NOTES:

NOTES: